LIFE CYCLE OF A DOG

By Kirsty Holmes

Words that look like **this** can be found in the glossary on page 24.

BookLife PUBLISHING

©2021
BookLife Publishing Ltd.
King's Lynn, Norfolk PE30 4LS

ISBN: 978-1-83927-474-9

All rights reserved.
Printed in Malta.

All facts, statistics, web addresses and URLs in this book were verified as valid and accurate at time of writing. No responsibility for any changes to external websites or references can be accepted by either the author or publisher.

Written by:
Kirsty Holmes

Edited by:
Shalini Vallepur

Designed by:
Lydia Williams

A catalogue record for this book is available from the British Library.

PHOTO CREDITS

Front Cover – 1 – stephan kerkhofs, 3DMI. 2 – ValSN. 3 – Eric Isselee, Tiplyashina Evgeniya, ictor Jiang. 4 – Tatiana Katsai, Syda Productions, Lopolov. 5 – Flamingo Images, Aila Images, digitalskillet. 6 – Eric Isselee. 7 – Pedro Gutierrez. 8 – Nina Buday. 9 – Tiplyashina Evgeniya. 10 – Helga Yastrebova23, art nick. 11 – Jackie Neff. 12 – Zenobillis. 13 – ThamKC. 14 – Master1305. 15 – ValSN. 16 – wavebreakmedia. 17 – Africa Studio, BIGANDT.COM, Victor Jiang, Pandas. 18 & 19 – Sascha Christian, chaoss, Masarik, Richard Chaff. 20 – Cavan-Images. 21 – mantinov. 22 & 23 – Eric Isselee. Images are courtesy of Shutterstock.com. With thanks to Getty Images, Thinkstock Photo and iStockphoto.

LIFE CYCLE OF A DOG

Page 4 — **What Is a Life Cycle?**
Page 6 — **Darling Dogs**
Page 8 — **Paw-fect Pregnancy**
Page 10 — **Precious Puppies**
Page 12 — **Jumping Juveniles**
Page 14 — **Delightful Dogs!**
Page 16 — **Life as a Dog**
Page 18 — **Fun Facts about Dogs**
Page 20 — **The End of Life as a Dog**
Page 22 — **The Life Cycle**
Page 24 — **Glossary and Index**

WHAT IS A LIFE CYCLE?

All living things have a life cycle. They are all born, they all grow bigger and their bodies change.

Baby

Child

Toddler

When they are fully grown, they have **offspring** of their own. In the end, all living things die. This is the life cycle.

DARLING DOGS

Dogs are **mammals**. They have four legs and a tail. Most dogs are covered in fur. Dogs have wet noses, and pads on their feet.

Fur

Wet Nose

Tail

Paws

Claws

Dogs can smell things from very far away.

Different breeds of dog are good at different things.

Doberman Pinscher

Pomeranian

Dogs are **domestic** animals. This means they can live with humans. Dogs come in all shapes and sizes. These different types are called breeds.

PAW-FECT PREGNANCY

A mother dog carries her babies in her belly before they are born. This is called pregnancy. Dogs are pregnant for around 63 days.

Can you see this mother's **swollen** belly?

A group of puppies born to the same mother at the same time is called a litter.

Some breeds of dog only have one or two puppies at a time. But some breeds can have lots – even as many as ten!

PRECIOUS PUPPIES

Puppies are born with their eyes and ears closed. This means they cannot see or hear. They stay with their mother to keep warm.

By the time they are a few weeks old, their eyes and ears open. They can stand and run around. They love to play!

JUMPING JUVENILES

By the time they are six months old, the puppies will be bigger, and some may look like their parents. Their fur will have grown, too.

This is called the juvenile stage. At this age, puppies grow very quickly, and will soon reach their adult size.

Puppies learn about the world around them by exploring, playing, smelling and licking.

DELIGHTFUL DOGS!

When the puppy is fully grown, it is an adult dog. Adult dogs all look different. Dogs can look like one of their parents, or a mixture of the two.

Adult dogs are ready to find a **mate** and have babies of their own. Female dogs will look after their puppies as they grow.

This mother is playing with her baby.

LIFE AS A DOG

Do you have a pet dog?

Dogs eat mostly meat, although they can eat some vegetables too. Most dogs live with humans, as pets.

Some dogs are working dogs. Dogs are very clever and can do a lot of different jobs to help us.

FUN FACTS ABOUT DOGS

A dog's noseprint is **unique** – just like a human fingerprint!

Most adult dogs have 42 teeth.

Dogs hang their tongues out and **pant** to cool down.

The Mexican hairless dog has no hair! Some of them may have a little hair on their head or tail.

THE END OF LIFE AS A DOG

Some dogs get grey hairs as they get older — just like people do.

Dogs live for around 7 to 15 years, but this might be longer or shorter depending on the breed.

Dogs slow down as they get older, and you might need to be gentler and quieter around them. Older dogs might sleep more and like to snuggle. Some might prefer to be left alone.

THE LIFE CYCLE

A dog's life cycle has different stages. Each stage looks very different from the last.

Juvenile

Adult Dog

The puppy is born with its eyes and ears closed. The juvenile puppy changes into an adult dog, and then the adult dog has offspring of its own.

In the end, the dog dies, and the life cycle is complete.

GLOSSARY

domestic when an animal is tame and can be kept by humans

mammals animals that are warm-blooded, have a backbone and make milk to feed their children

mate a partner (of the same species) that an animal chooses to have young with

offspring the babies of an animal or plant

pant to take short, quick breaths

swollen larger than normal

unique unlike anything or anyone else

INDEX

babies 4, 8, 15
breeds 7, 9, 20
fur 6, 12

hearing 10
litters 9
play 11, 13, 15

puppies 9–10, 12–15, 22–23
smell 6, 13